ADVERTISING TO CHILDREN

Essential Viewpoints

ADVERTISING TO
CHILDREN

BY MARCIA AMIDON LUSTED

Content Consultant
Mary McIlrath, PhD
Marketing Researcher

ABDO
Publishing Company

CREDITS

Published by ABDO Publishing Company, 8000 West 78th Street, Edina, Minnesota 55439. Copyright © 2009 by Abdo Consulting Group, Inc. International copyrights reserved in all countries. No part of this book may be reproduced in any form without written permission from the publisher. The Essential Library™ is a trademark and logo of ABDO Publishing Company.

Printed in the United States.

Editor: Patricia Stockland
Copy Editor: Paula Lewis
Interior Design and Production: Ryan Haugen
Cover Design: Nicole Brecke

Library of Congress Cataloging-in-Publication Data
Lusted, Marcia Amidon.
  Advertising to children / by Marcia Amidon Lusted.
    p. cm. — (Essential viewpoints)
  Includes bibliographical references and index.
  ISBN 978-1-60453-107-7
  1. Advertising and children—Juvenile literature. 2. Child consumers—Juvenile literature. I. Title.

  HF5829.L873 2009
  659.1083—dc22

                          2008006990

TABLE OF CONTENTS

Today's young consumer has enormous spending power that attracts marketers.

MARKETING 101

Every day, from the moment we wake up and turn on the radio or television to the last magazine we read or Internet site we visit at night, we are exposed to advertising. And for those between the ages of one and twenty, much of the advertising is tailored specifically to products that interest them. Young children and teens once were considered just a small part of the family unit by advertisers. But since the early 1980s, advertisers have discovered children and teens make up an enormous market. They not only have money to spend but also influence the purchases their families make. In her book *Consuming Kids,* Susan Linn describes her family's experience:

> *My daughter is a popular kid these days. Taco Bell wants her, and so does Burger King. Abercrombie and Fitch has a whole store devoted to her. Pert Plus has a shampoo she'll love. Ethan Allen is creating bedroom sets she can't live without. Alpo even wants to sell her dog food.*[1]

Today's child, preteen, and teen view approximately 40,000 commercials a year on television—twice as many as they would have seen in the 1970s. This accounts for 16 percent of their total viewing time. The Internet sites they visit also carry advertising, as do their cell phones. Advertising does not take a break during the school day. Students may watch a school television network that was provided for free but also contains commercials that are viewed by the classes. They might buy their lunch

In 1983, Congress regulated children's television by passing the Children's Television Education Act. In 1984, television advertising was deregulated. This meant the Federal Trade Commission (FTC) could no longer place limitations on advertising. Program-length commercials were no longer banned, and kids could watch cartoons that critics claimed were basically toy advertisements.

Advertising crept into every aspect of children's lives. Enola Aird of The Motherhood Project said, "A lot of really smart marketers discovered children as a huge market. . . . So the philosophy becomes 'Let's get to them early. Let's get to them often. Let's get to them as many places as we can get to them. And our goal is not just to sell them products and services, but to turn them into lifelong consumers.'"[2]

from a Pizza Hut franchise inside their school. Banners advertising school events may display a soft-drink company's logo.

Even the trendy clothing that kids wear promotes the manufacturers' brands with logos or easily identified styling. At an early age, kids have been made aware of the latest video game or the hottest new MP3 player—even the best cars. Once they get home from school, they may reach for a snack that has been packaged and marketed especially for them. The advertising begins again with every television program they watch or Web page they view. Advertising is big business where kids are concerned. And advertisers are increasingly aware of how important kids and teens are to the market.

SPENDING POWER

Why have children become such big business for advertisers and the

Even children as young as three years old can identify brand names, such as the Littlest Pet Shop.

clients they represent? Companies want to attract children and teens because of their enormous spending power. Businesses want this group to spend those dollars on their products. One market-research group estimated that U.S. teens spent more than $159 billion in 2005. This represents a combination of money they had earned themselves, money they received as gifts, and spending money from their parents.

Martin Lindstrom's book, *BRANDchild*, is an extensive marketing study about kids and their relationship to brand names. According to Lindstrom:

> No other generation has ever had as much disposable income as this one. So it's no coincidence that this emerging generation has become powerful enough to have a specific allotment in every marketing director's budget. They spend money and time with a casual and carefree attitude: they get what they want when they want it.[3]

Kid Income

Kids are a popular market because they have dollars to spend on the things they like. But where do kids get their money? According to James McNeal in *The Kids' Market: Myths and Realities,* the major sources of income for kids are:

- Allowances: 45 percent
- Household work: 21 percent
- Gifts from parents: 16 percent
- Work outside the home: 10 percent
- Gifts from others: 8 percent

THE BASICS OF MARKETING

On the surface, marketing seems like a very basic idea. A company has a product, shows it to people, and they buy it. But it is not that simple, especially when there are more products to choose from than consumers have money for.

Initially, advertisers approached children with the same marketing strategies used for adults. The basic principles of marketing address four areas: product,

price, place, and promotion. First, there must be
a product or service to sell. This must be clear and
easy to understand so that the buyer knows exactly
what the company is offering. The company then
establishes a product price that is reasonable and
competitive with other similar products. Place means
choosing a method of advertising that will best reach
the targeted market. Promotion is communicating
with potential customers to make them feel that
they are making the right choice by choosing that
product.

Advertising and marketing companies assemble
test groups of people drawn from a certain age or
demographic to evaluate products. Surveys might
be used to obtain consumers' opinions on existing
products and ideas for new products. These methods
help marketers follow consumer trends. Effective
marketing also convinces consumers that buying
those products will enhance their looks, intelligence,
or popularity.

To draw attention to their products, advertisers
traditionally used television commercials, print
advertisements in newspapers and magazines,
billboards, and even contests and giveaways. But
marketing has become more than just creating a

product and making it available for sale. Companies strive to develop a loyalty to their product or brand name. This loyalty will keep the consumer buying their products in the future. Advertisers also encourage consumerism by showing people items to spend their money on that they did not even know they wanted or needed.

Catering to a Tough Market

Marketing specifically to kids and teens has meant developing many new methods for reaching such a changeable audience. Advertisers have used new technologies, such as the Internet and cell phones, as well as the ever-elusive power of "coolness" to sell their products to kids and teens. As a result, advertising has grown to encompass almost every part of the day for children. This includes what food they eat, the clothes they wear, and the movies they watch. Often, these are linked together in one big, layered marketing effort. As a result, kids are more aware of brand names than ever before.

Heart of the Controversy

Is the concept of marketing and advertising specifically to children and teens negative or positive? Does it empower kids by giving them choices and making their voices important in consumerism and to the economy? Or is the enormous amount of marketing aimed at kids that creates materialistic, overstimulated youth who will face a lifetime of debt? In her book, *Born to Buy*, Juliet Schor wrote:

> *Kids and teens are now the epicenter of American consumer culture. They command the attention, creativity, and dollars of advertisers. Their tastes drive market trends. Their opinions shape brand strategies. Yet few adults recognize the*

The Motherhood Project

On Mother's Day 2000, a group from the Institute for American Values, known as the Motherhood Project, issued a statement to advertisers. Concerned about the growing impact of advertising and marketing upon children, their "Watch Out for Children" statement spoke directly to marketers. It called attention to their concerns and what they wanted done:

For us, children are priceless gifts. For you, our children are customers, and childhood is a "market segment" to be exploited. We are alarmed by the mounting evidence . . . that marketing to children is harming them. In pursuit of the market for children and youth, you are aggressively extending your reach, going after age groups that until recently have been considered off limits, and occupying more and more of our children's psychic and physical space. . . . The line between meeting and creating consumer needs and desires is increasingly being crossed, as your battery of highly trained and creative experts study, analyze, persuade, and manipulate our children. The evidence of harm to our children's physical, cognitive, and social health, to their values, and to their emotional well-being is overwhelming.[4]

magnitude of this shift and its consequences for the futures of our children and of our culture.[5]

Many experts in child development are disturbed by the trend of consumerism among young people. In a 2001 statement to advertisers, the Motherhood Project of the Institute for American Values stated, "More and more, the culture seems to teach that a good life is a materially successful life, and that a primary goal of life is to garner material possessions."[6]

Marketers note, though, that kids are empowered by being given a voice in product development. Through this, they learn to be savvy consumers. As Gene del Vecchio says in Juliet Schor's book *Born to Buy*,

> *Kids have very little control over the world in which they live. Therefore, they love to gain a measure of control over their sphere of existence. . . . Control touches a strong need that children have to be independent.*[7]

The opportunity to make choices builds independence and self-esteem. It also promotes the feeling of being part of a peer group. This may be especially important for teens struggling with personal identity and feeling alienated and different

*Young consumers appreciate having a choice of products.
Not everyone agrees with this extensive product exposure, however.*

from others. Shared experiences with video games, music, and Internet sites bring teens together.

Kids and teens have also learned that they have a say in what these companies produce. They are important because of the way they choose to spend their dollars. By earning and spending money, they are making a major contribution to the economy. Consumerism also creates a need for workers to produce goods, which adds employment opportunities.

Marketers point to other benefits of advertising, such as television programs that viewers do not have to pay for because the ads cover the cost of the programming. Marketers also attest that advertising creates better products. If products are going to attract and keep consumers, they must constantly improve. While these are not benefits specific to kids and teens as consumers, they do benefit society overall.

Only by exploring both sides of the debate is it possible to decide if kids benefit from advertising or if it is only another path by which companies can profit. Everyone likes to have choices in what they eat, wear, and buy. But is so much choice always a good thing? Or is it one of the accepted benefits of living in a free-market economy?

Rename That Landmark

One of the most obvious signs of the extent to which advertising has affected everyday life is the trend for large corporations to buy "naming rights" to landmarks such as baseball parks and arenas. The stadium home of the Washington Redskins became FedEx Field, and San Francisco's famous Candlestick Park stadium became 3Com Park. However, after many complaints from the public, San Francisco bought back the naming rights from the corporate sponsor and returned the field's original name. It was the first city to reverse the naming trend.

Some products, such as slime, are created specifically for kids.

Comic books were collectibles that included ads targeted at kids.

A History of Kids
as Consumers

*P*roducts for children, including books
and clothing, have existed for hundreds
of years. Even in the 1870s, certain toys such as dolls
were status symbols for the children wealthy enough
to own them. Later generations became buyers,

collectors, and traders of products such as baseball cards, comic books, and stuffed animals. They also bought books and movie tickets. These are all early examples of marketing to kids.

Even though companies realized that kids were avid consumers of certain products, they were not considered to be a big market on their own or to have much money to spend. Therefore, most of the advertising relied on appealing to mothers to buy products for their children rather than addressing kids directly. Advertisers would display products that were good for children, such as bread enriched with vitamins and minerals or milk enhanced with vitamin D. They also promoted certain products, including books and games with educational content. These tactics encouraged mothers to purchase the products to make their children healthier and enhance their well-being.

Eventually, this type of marketing shifted into something often called "pester power." Beginning with radio serials, which were series programs on the radio, advertisers began using tactics to get kids to pester their parents to buy them certain items. This evolved to cereals with a prize in the box or a toy that they saw in a commercial. Advertisers were not really approaching kids directly because they realized that the parents controlled the cash necessary for purchases. But marketing was beginning to address children more directly. This became possible partly because advertisers had direct access to kids through children's television programs.

Pester power became even more effective as family dynamics shifted. As more parents held full-time jobs and had less time to spend with their children, they more often made guilt purchases. According to Juliet Schor, "Time-starved households have become easy prey for marketers, whose research shows that parents who spend less time with their children will spend more money on them."[1] Pester power has

---

The Comic Book Controversy

Beginning in the 1930s and 1940s, comic books were one of the first products to be linked specifically to and marketed for child consumers. But similar to many of today's video games, comic books were also the first product to be blamed for negative affects on children, namely violence and sex.

In the early 1950s, psychiatrist Fredric Werther published a book titled *Seduction of the Innocent*. In it, he basically blamed comic books for juvenile delinquency and crime. As a result of the book and the comic book controversy, a Comic Code was created. Under this code, many comic books (especially those with "terror" and "horror" in the titles) could no longer be published.

However, the restrictions on comic books and the public's perception of them as bad for kids were actually strong publicity. The more adults complained about these products, the more appealing they became to kids.

now evolved into a situation where
kids influence an enormous amount
of the spending that takes place in
their households. This pertains to
food, clothing, and entertainment,
as well as larger purchases including
technology and cars. Kids are also
being raised by parents who grew up
in an increasingly consumer-driven
atmosphere.

E.T. Embedded

In 1982, the movie *E.T.: The Extra-Terrestrial* made its debut with the first example of embedded marketing. In the movie, the main character uses Reese's Pieces candy to entice the alien into his house. This was one of the first times that a product was prominently positioned in a movie. The sale of Reese's Pieces increased by 66 percent.

THE MARKETING MACHINE TAKES OFF

Another milestone in the history of marketing
to children occurred in 1976 with the release of the
movie *Star Wars*. Movies that appealed to younger
audiences sold an enormous amount of tickets.
This led to movie tie-in products, such as action
figures, clothing, and even bed sheets and wallpaper.
Advertisers realized that if kids liked a movie, tie-in
products would be particularly popular.

In 1978, the Federal Trade Commission (FTC)
tried to impose regulations on ads aimed specifically
at children. Congress, however, blocked its attempts
because it felt the FTC's term "unfair advertising"
was too vague. As a result, there were no government

More than three decades after its first release,
Star Wars and its tie-in products are still popular.

regulations on how products could be marketed
to kids. With this, advertising for children took
off. Realizing the need for a set of policies and
procedures, the industry created its own regulations.
Both the Better Business Bureau (BBB) and the
Children's Advertising Review Unit (CARU) created
rules for the industry to follow. As CARU notes on
its Web site, they work together:

. . . in voluntary cooperation with children's advertisers to ensure that advertising messages directed to young children are truthful, accurate and sensitive to their particular audience, thereby preserving their freedom to direct their messages to young children.[2]

In the 1980s, most marketing was directed at adults, especially those who fell into the age category of "baby boomers," simply because there were so many of them. Then the number of teenagers in the United States increased for the first time since the 1970s. By the 1990s, advertisers began to recognize that children and teens were a massive market in their own right. At the same time, the economic recession of the late 1980s and early 1990s affected the country. The only product areas not affected by the recession were those where teens and kids made the most

Conforming Nonconformists

Some of the trends in fashion that appeared in the 1970s and 1980s began as teen attempts to protest against consumer capitalism. These alternative styles, such as the punk movement, began as reactions to standard fashion trends but ended up becoming trends themselves. The nonconformist styles eventually became the conformists' fashion trends.

Cereals with cartoon kid appeal are often at the center of the advertising debate.

purchases. Naomi Klein, author of the book *No Logo*, observed:

> This was not a time for selling Tide and Snuggle to housewives—it was a time for beaming MTV, Nike, Hilfiger, Microsoft, Netscape and Wired to global teens and their overgrown imitators. Their parents may have gone bargain-basement, but kids, it turned out, were still willing to pay up to fit in. [3]

Peer pressure developed as a powerful marketing force among teens and even younger kids.

The New Product Category

With so much spending power, kids and teens created their own market in areas that had previously catered to adults. From clothing to foods to personal-hygiene products such as soap, shampoo, and cosmetics, everything could now be made in kid-appealing formats. Foods were made in different colors and shapes, such as purple ketchup or dinosaur-shaped chicken nuggets. Shampoo was packaged in bottles with caps shaped like cartoon characters. Sunscreen was manufactured to come out of the bottle as a green lotion, although the color would disappear once applied to the skin. Eventually, even higher-priced items such as computers and cell phones were made in versions with colors, designs, and features that appealed to young consumers.

Cereal Characters

Cartoon characters have been used to sell cereals since the 1940s. Characters such as Snap, Crackle, and Pop (Kellogg's Rice Krispies) and Tony the Tiger (Kellogg's Frosted Flakes) have helped sell cereal to generations of kids. They continue to do so today, although their appearance is frequently adjusted to keep up with popular culture. However, they are the first targets in a continuing controversy about whether it is appropriate to use cartoon characters (including SpongeBob SquarePants and Disney's princesses) to sell foods to kids.

The trend of creating kid-specific versions of adult products and brands soon spread to creating new stores. Popular adult stores such as The Gap and Pottery Barn created Baby Gap and Pottery Barn Kids. Restaurants discovered the monetary value of creating environments just for children, such as indoor playgrounds.

Advertisers also want to tie into the elusive "cool factor." When something becomes a highly sought-after fad that is a ticket to social success, kids buy it. This can be a certain brand name, place, or activity. It may start with something like a Webkinz stuffed animal or a video gaming system such as X-Box or Wii. Social status has become a direct result of consumerism. Kids can identify with a group based on what brands or products they favor. Most kid consumers believe that if they arrive at school with the latest popular item or clothing, they will be admired and envied. Marketers then create these products that appeal to kids and set them apart from adults.

The evolution of marketing to children has resulted in kids and teens wielding an enormous amount of marketing power. According to Susan Linn:

Corporations are racing to stake their claim on the consumer group formerly known as children. What was once the purview of a few entertainment and toy companies has escalated into a gargantuan, multi-tentacled enterprise with a combined marketing budget estimated at over $15 billion annually. Children are the darlings of corporate America. They're targets for marketers of everything from hamburgers to minivans. [4]

A Continuing Process

Marketing to children is also a process that changes constantly in order to provide the newest and the best must-have products. Cereal box prizes and television commercials can no longer get the job done. Advertisers have had to change and adapt their methods in order to reach this ever-changing group in as many different ways as possible. The CEO of a major marketing group explains:

In today's world, many marketers are finding that their tried and tested "rules" no longer always apply. Across all segments, social relationships are changing, media is fragmenting, and everything is happening at warp speed. But it is amongst tomorrow's consumers that the changes are having the most impact. [5]

Today's savvy consumer culture has grown up saturated with advertising, commercials, and brand loyalty. Successful marketing requires an entirely new system of researching the needs and, more importantly, the wants, of kids and teens. Entirely new methods for attracting these young consumers are also needed.

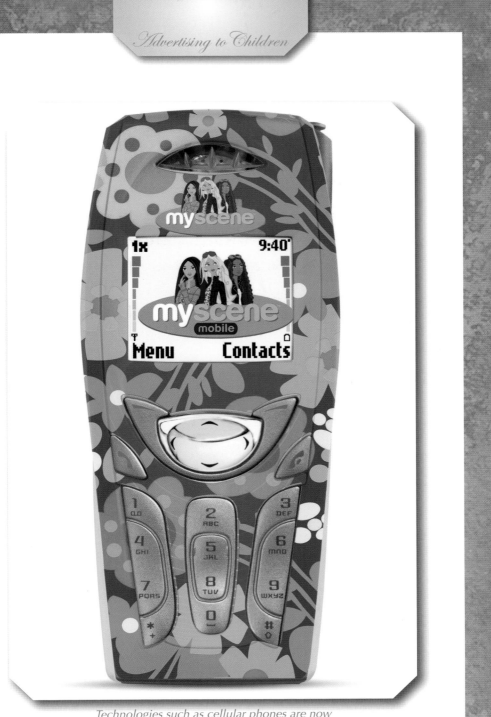

Technologies such as cellular phones are now designed with young consumers in mind.

*Researchers categorize young buyers so that products
can be directly built for and marketed to them.*

MARKETING TO
KIDS TODAY

ost kids and teens do not realize that advertisers have categorized them as one of four types of consumers. Marketers can even predict what specific basic values drive kids and teens to buy what they buy.

LET US TELL YOU WHO YOU ARE

Market researchers tailor products to their intended audience. They have identified four specific personality types. These types not only determine to whom a product should be marketed but also how that product can catch on, become the next big thing, and spread among the groups. The four groups identified by marketers are edges, persuaders, followers, and reflexives.

Edges are those who do not follow the rules. They do not like to think of themselves as ordinary and certainly do not think that they follow fashions and trends. They might like to participate in extreme sports, usually do not do their schoolwork, and are rarely at home. But edges are an important part of the marketer's profile. Martin Lindstrom explains:

> Because they break the rules and run their own lives, they are perceived as independent trendsetters. They try products long before everyone else—and they often combine old products in new ways, re-inventing them and making them cool.[1]

Product Placement

In the 2002 James Bond movie, *Die Another Day*, the moviemakers collected approximately $160 million in fees to show products such as British Airways, Finlandia vodka, Heineken beer, and Sony electronics in the movie. In another James Bond movie, the Philip Morris tobacco company paid more than $350,000 just to have the Bond character smoke Lark cigarettes. In the movie *Baby Boom*, Huggies diapers paid filmmakers $100,000 to show its product in the movie.

Marketers know that persuaders will make a trend popular.

Persuaders are those who are seen as cool and who pick up new trends the fastest. Persuaders are not as rebellious as the edges, and other kids are more likely to follow their lead. Concerned with their appearance, persuaders always want to look good. When a persuader decides to wear a certain type of clothing or buys a particular product, others who want to be cool and popular will do the same. Persuaders are who the less popular kids want to be. And persuaders are the marketer's dream because whatever they have, others will soon want as well.

Most kids are classified as followers. These are the average kids, the ones who are not really popular or cool. They do not have as much self-esteem as edges and persuaders. They are never the first to try something new, but once it becomes popular, they will adopt it. They are followers instead of leaders. Because the followers comprise a major portion of kids, it is important for marketers to reach them.

The reflexives are those who are on the outside of the popular groups and are likely to remain there even though they try to be socially accepted and popular. They, too, do not have a lot of self-esteem. Even though they try to fit in with the other groups, they do not usually pick up on fashion trends and are not as likely to go out with groups of friends. Since the reflexives have minimal influence on their peers, marketers intentionally try to avoid messages or images that would appeal to this group.

Product Placement Pop-ups?

Filmmakers are required to disclose to their audience that paid product placements are visible in their movie. Because these announcements are usually listed in the credits and easily overlooked, some consumer commercial-alerting organizations feel that paid placement should be more obvious. Some even want to see pop-ups to inform the viewer every time a paid placement appears on the screen. Advertisers argue that product placement is obvious and additional notifications within pop-ups are unnecessary.

Marketers use these four categories to help determine the best possible group to approach with a particular brand or product. Not every kid fits neatly into one of these four categories. But enough do so that marketers can speak to an enormous number of young shoppers simply by targeting a particular group.

Why Do You Want It?

Marketers know what specific groups to target with their advertising. They also know why kids buy what they buy. Marketers have identified core values that influence every buying decision kids make: fear, fantasy, mastery, humor, and love.

A value such as fear might make a video game with thrills and violence appealing. Fantasy might be the reason why a child is drawn to a castle-building set. They want to use their imagination and create a world totally different from their everyday life. Mastery fits in with teens' desires to rule their own worlds. It might drive them to reach the highest level of an X-Box 360 game. Humor is the reason why kids like movies that make fun of adults and show characters doing crazy things. This is especially true if the humor appeals to kids and is not something adults find funny. Love is the value behind a child's need for dolls that they can take care of and cherish. This also applies to stuffed animals, such as Webkinz.

Marketers link these core values to three drivers, or motivations: the mirror effect, gaming ability, and collection value. The mirror effect occurs when a child wants to imitate the grown-up world. Gaming ability is a way to succeed among other kids by how well the child can play a game, make high scores, or beat levels. Collection value is the driver behind collecting things such as trading cards or Beanie Babies—the bigger the collection, the more admiration from other kids.

Marketers can combine these values and drivers with the types of kids most likely to buy a product and make it a trend.

Tweening and KAGOY

Identifying buyer personality types and purchase drivers has been used for years. But there are new aspects to consider when marketing to today's kids. Children are growing up more quickly than their parents did.

Books or Commercials?

Product placement is no longer limited to movies and television shows. In 1992, the *M&M Counting Book* was published. It included pictures of the candies to help teach counting. It has sold more than 1 million copies. Since then, more counting and math concept books have appeared using products such as Goldfish crackers, Fruit Loops cereal, Oreo cookies, and Hershey's chocolate bars.

Products that once appealed to teens are now being marketed to their much younger siblings. Juliet Schor gives an example in her book *Born to Buy*,

GIA

One of the companies directly involved in using kids for viral marketing about products is Girls Intelligence Agency (GIA). GIA recruits girls between the ages of 8 and 18 to talk about and create interest in certain products. GIA girls receive new product samples to test with their friends. Then, they report back to the company with their friends' reactions to those products. Girls also text and e-mail each other about products and are urged to be "sly" in collecting information for GIA about their friends' preferences. According to the GIA Web site, they are

a unique organization comprised of approximately 40,000 "Secret Agents," ages 8 to 29, living all over the United States. GIA communicates with these Influencers daily, seeking out their opinions, ideas, motivations, dreams, and goals, and translates that information to help hundreds of corporations in the U.S. to strategically reach and connect with the female youth market.[3]

GIA creates trust with its agents and then uses the information it collects from them to help corporate clients develop marketing aimed specifically at this market.

Twenty years ago, Seventeen magazine targeted sixteen year olds; now it aims at eleven and twelves. In a telling gesture, the toy industry has officially lowered its upper age target from fourteen to ten.[2]

Now, toy manufacturers feel that kids are done playing with toys at the age of ten. Kids are ready to move into the world of fashion, makeup, Internet gaming, and relationships with the opposite sex. Kids identify themselves with the adult world at earlier and earlier ages. Marketers have created a phrase for this: Kids Are Getting Older Younger (KAGOY). An action figure that once would have been marketed to 12-year-old boys is now targeted to 7-year-old boys instead. Girls are leaving dolls and looking toward fashion, makeup, and teen celebrities at much earlier ages. Marketing has adjusted as a result.

Another tactic marketers use to deal with this is called "tweening." The term *tween* refers to the age group between kids and teens, a group that once was not separately identified. As younger kids want to be treated like older kids at an earlier age, the tween category has grown as a way to handle this transition group. Tweening is the marketing of products and entertainment that were once thought suitable for teens to younger and younger kids. If a child in kindergarten comes home wanting a T-shirt with the name of a popular rock star on it, chances are he or she has been targeted by tweening.

Marketing to tweens is an increasingly important part of marketing to kids as a whole. In *The Great Tween Buying Machine*, author David Siegel comments that tweens are the center of the kid market:

Too old to be a kid, too young to be a teen. Too old to want to be totally dependent on parents, too young to have a work permit, tweens can create a [very powerful] brand.[4]

VIRAL MARKETING

With marketers readily identifying their target markets, what new methods have they developed to reach these potential consumers? One is called "viral marketing." It is a way of "infecting" kid consumers with the desire for a particular brand or product by infiltrating every aspect of their experiences with it.

Viral marketing originally described the way that marketers would go into Internet chat rooms and pretend to be other kids talking about how great a particular product is. According to Martin Lindstrom:

> *Viral marketing characteristically includes a message, which is adopted and transmitted by the audience themselves. We're all engaged in viral communication. Think of the jokes, the images, the chain letters and anecdotes sent by friends and family members based all over the world.*[5]

Viral marketing works the same way. Like a virus, this type of communication spreads uncontrollably and soon every kid wants to have the product.

The continuing word-of-mouth advertising markets the product without further effort. This is also called peer-to-peer marketing because tween and teen leaders will adopt a product or a brand and spread it to their peers and then to the rest of their community.

Along with viral marketing, advertisers will also embed, or place, products in movies, video games, and television shows. This is an effective way to market a product without actually appearing to. Actors may be drinking a particular brand of soda or enjoying coffee at one of the major coffee chains. It extends to actors playing a video game where the brand name is evident and scenery in the game shows billboards displaying ads. Each of these is an example of embedded product ads.

Partnerships

Partnerships have been created between established organizations and products. The Girl Scouts began offering a "Fashion Adventure" overnight mall shopping experience in conjunction with the Limited Too clothing store for girls. Groups such as the Boys and Girls Clubs and even the National Parent-Teacher Association form partnerships with marketing companies as a way to recruit children's opinions on certain products.

THE "COOL" FACTOR

Nearly every form of marketing to kids has come to rely on the "cool" factor. If a company can create a buzz for its product, get the persuader kids to notice it and adopt it, and turn it into a trend or a must-have item, it has succeeded in creating cool. If something is seen as the new cool thing to own, and a child's popularity and sense of belonging to their peer group hinges on having that cool item, they will find a way to buy it. Cool is elusive; once kids discard a brand name, a game, or a gadget, there is little chance that it will become popular again. As consumers, kids have lots of cash to spend, but they are also quick to move on to the next cool thing. Understanding and creating the next cool item is so important to marketers that companies specializing in advertising to kids have held conferences on understanding cool.

By looking at the different methods that advertisers use to figure out purchasing decisions, it is easy to see how they can convince kids to spend money on the newest cool thing. But targeted marketing to kids for these kinds of products is just part of what advertisers do well. Not only do they want to persuade consumers to spend their money on products, but they also want to influence what and when consumers eat.

The latest video game is often the newest cool thing.

Many foods are altered or packaged to appeal to kids.

Food Marketing

*I*t might seem like the simplest thing in the world: when people are hungry, they go to the kitchen and find something to eat, or perhaps go out to a restaurant for a meal. But for kids today, there is an entire system in place to subtly direct just what they want to eat, and when and where they will eat it.

SATURATED WITH FOOD MARKETING

The media has reported that many of today's kids are overweight or obese and addicted to high-fat, high-calorie fast foods and snacks. Part of the blame is placed on a sedentary lifestyle. Many children spend more time watching television or playing video games than going outside to play and get exercise. Some people blame part of the problem on tremendous amounts of food marketing.

Fast-food companies such as McDonald's and Burger King, as well as food companies that produce snack foods and soft drinks, spend millions of dollars every year on advertising that specifically targets children. And most young children cannot see the difference between the show and a commercial. Susan Linn states in *Consuming Kids*,

Fast Food Nation

In 2001, author Eric Schlosser published *Fast Food Nation*. This book exposed the darker side of fast-food marketing and how unhealthy the products can be. The book became a movie, followed by the 2004 documentary *Supersize Me*, directed by Morgan Spurlock. For 30 days, Spurlock ate only McDonald's food and documented the effects it had on his health. In 2005, an enhanced version of the documentary was created for use in school health curriculums.

According to one study, kids watching Saturday morning television are exposed to one food commercial every five minutes. Almost all of these are for foods high in calories, fat, salt, and/or sugar. [And] most of the movies and many of the TV programs children watch are marketed with off-screen food promotions. [1]

Marketers are trying to create situations where consumers are constantly exposed to their brand names. Products are displayed in as many places as possible, whether it is on the grocery-store shelf, in a television cartoon, or on the cover of a book.

The most successful food marketing has been to create an entirely new category of foods that appeal strictly to kids. These food items are generally tied to familiar characters and entertainment or are practically toys themselves.

Play with Your Food

Parents are often persuaded to buy foods because of important nutrients that are healthy for their children. But advertisers are drawing on the idea that kids want to eat foods that their parents would never eat, such as high-sugar, brightly colored candies and drinks. This theory reinforces the marketing

SpongeBob SquarePants has been accused of enticing children to "play with their food."

idea of "adults versus kids," and that kids will either pester their parents to buy a food product or buy it themselves simply because it sets them apart from adults.

Food marketing attempts to maximize the notion that food is fun. According to Susan Linn:

> The food industry refers to the phenomenon as "eatertainment." Food commercials aimed at children don't talk as much about "great taste" as they do about having fun—associating food with action, friends, excitement.[2]

This is known in the advertising industry as "trans-toying." It began when everyday products were turned into toys. Items such as toothbrushes, shampoo, and adhesive bandages were decorated with licensed cartoon characters. Bandages looked like tattoos and shampoo bottles were given a plastic character head.

The trans-toying concept has spread to foods as well. These include green and purple ketchup and cereals that turn milk blue. Hot water poured over oatmeal reveals brightly colored candy pieces and cheese snacks turn a person's mouth and tongue different colors. These made food more of a plaything than a source of nutrition. Critics worry that kids will never appreciate wholesome, regular food. Juliet B. Shor argues that

> [m]arketers would have us believe that the purpose of food is to play with it. Isn't that an obscene value, when there are people in the world who are starving?[3]

Connecting food to television shows and even holidays is another method of enticing kids to either buy it or ask for it. Many products come in special versions with cartoon characters from shows that attract children and make them want the product. Movie characters appear on boxes of cereal and special editions of soda to attract younger purchasers. Special foods tied to holidays also get attention from kids, such as Oreos with orange filling for Halloween or cereal with special marshmallow shapes or red- and green-colored pieces for Christmas.

CORRECTING ITSELF

Because of these advertising efforts, the industry has created new initiatives to regulate itself and set limits on what is an appropriate level of advertising for food. In 2005, the Federal Trade Commission (FTC) asked industry regulators such as the Better Business Bureau (BBB) and the Children's Advertising Review Unit (CARU) to address the obesity epidemic among U.S. children. Advertisers responded to these requests and set forth new guidelines in considering the cognitive abilities of children and the truthfulness and accuracy of food-advertising messages.

Internet Food Games

One way that food companies keep kids interacting with their brand names is to create games on their company Web sites. Kids play these games that either feature characters made of food products (such as Hostess's Twinkie the Kid) or allow kids to drive cars with food logos. The Nabisco site allows kids to shoot chocolate chips into cookies with a Chip Blaster.

*The Teenie Beanie Baby promotion at McDonald's
was a huge hit among both kid and adult collectors.*

WHAT IS CHILDHOOD WITHOUT A HAPPY MEAL?

Some of the most aggressive and successful
advertising campaigns designed to attract kid
consumers are those created by fast-food companies.
McDonald's developed the Happy Meal to attract
children to their restaurants at a time when
younger consumers considered fast food boring.
McDonald's started by using games and puzzles as
a way to give kids something to play with while they
ate. Eventually, the companies began to include

a toy in the meal. The toys appeal to the collector aspect of behavior. One of the best examples of this was McDonald's Teenie Beanie Baby promotion in 1997. In ten days, McDonald's sold 100 million of these special Happy Meals simply because kids—and adults—wanted to collect the toys given away with the meals.

Cereal companies have been putting toys in their products for years. In many cases, the toys have become the most important part of the meal. But because the parent or child has to purchase the food in order to get the toy, the food sells.

Fast-food chains have also discovered that linking the toys in meals to current movies is another way to attract younger consumers. At one time, McDonald's had an agreement with the Walt Disney Company to produce Happy Meals tied to the current Disney movie. Kids would receive toys based on movie characters. This generated advertising for the movie and brought kids to the restaurants to get those toys, which usually changed every week for several months.

A Trustworthy Clown

McDonald's Ronald Mc-Donald clown is a marketing icon. Although he never actually tells kids that they should eat hamburgers and French fries, he makes kids feel good about McDonald's. Ronald connects with kids and makes his restaurant seem like a fun place.

Again, the collecting instinct made kids want to obtain the entire set of characters.

Marketing Food at School

One type of advertising occurs where kids spend a large portion of their day: school. Food in schools was once limited to just what was available in the school cafeteria. As schools grew larger and budgets were reduced, they had to turn to the opportunities offered by marketers for free materials and equipment in exchange for advertising.

Vending machines were the first opportunity to market foods

Coca-Cola Controversy

In 1998, a high school senior named Mike Cameron was suspended for wearing a Pepsi shirt during a Coke Day rally at his school. The student government had come up with the rally as a way to win a $10,000 prize being offered by the Coca-Cola company to the school that came up with the best way to distribute discount Coke coupons. To win the prize, students at the Greenbrier High School, dressed in red and white, lined up to spell out the word COKE for officials from the beverage company.

Mike Cameron got into trouble for wearing his Pepsi shirt while the Coke picture was taken. Administrators claim that he did it as a disruptive prank and not to make a statement about soda marketing in his school. According to an article in the Washington Post, Cameron said, "I don't consider this a prank. I like to be an individual. That's the way I am."[4] Cameron was widely interviewed by national media after his suspension and applauded by those who believed that schools should not be catering to soft drink companies.

that were not part of the cafeteria offerings. Sodas and snacks were available as an alternative to healthier cafeteria foods. Soda companies such as Coca-Cola and Pepsi competed for this business by offering schools deals called pouring contracts. A school would receive money in exchange for an exclusive contract to place that particular soda company's vending machines in the school. According to the National Soft Drink Association, 10 percent of all schools are paid for allowing only one brand of soda to be sold on their campus.

Pizza and Books

Pizza Hut's Book It program is an example of how advertisers use school curricula to promote their products. Students keep track of how many minutes they read daily. When they accumulate a certain amount of time, they earn a free personal pan pizza. Teachers receive materials from Pizza Hut that promote the program and the company's products. If students earn a free pizza every month during the school year, they receive a special medal at the end of the year.

Fast-food franchises have also increased their presence by operating stores inside some schools. Kids can buy Pizza Hut pizzas or Burger King's burgers and fries without leaving campus.

Marketing foods to kids inside their own schools is not limited to the actual availability of these foods. Food advertising appears in places such as Channel One, a free television network given to schools in exchange for allowing commercials to be represented on the channel, many of which are for soft drinks and snacks. Textbooks may have examples of math problems using grams of fat in a Burger King Whopper or the diameter of an Oreo cookie. Science teachers receive kits from food companies that teach physics and geology concepts using brand-name food and snack products.

Big food corporations also sponsor contests with large cash prizes for the winning school. While these contests generate much-needed money for schools, this form of advertising constantly keeps these products and brands in front of the kids.

Good or Bad?

Marketing is present in almost every aspect of a child's life. It can create a desire for a product that might not necessarily be the healthiest or best choice, or even something that the child or family can afford. But is marketing targeted specifically to kids always a bad thing? Or are there positive aspects that balance out the negatives?

Vending machines at schools often cause controversy among parents, students, and school boards.

*Young consumers know what they want,
and they want their opinions to be heard.*

CREATING SAVVY CONSUMERS

In many ways, both the advertisers and the target age-group feel that it is important to give young consumers their own voice. Parents and other adults used to determine what was appropriate for children and whether it was healthy or nutritious or educational. But with the advent of marketing campaigns targeted to kids, many have developed their own distinctive voice in the consumer culture.

With money to spend and power to influence their families' spending habits as well, kids are a growing consumer group. And marketers want to know what they think. Kids are brought together through focus groups where marketers are eager to learn just what kids want. They talk about and sample products as well as complete surveys about their opinions and buying habits. With such enormous spending power, the wants, needs, and preferences of kids and teens are taken seriously. More than ever, being a child no longer means being powerless and voiceless in advertising. It is not solely up to adults to determine what their choices are. The opinions and preferences of kids are eagerly sought and taken seriously, and this has empowered them as a group.

Advertisers are interested in what kids and teens want, making

Building Bears

One of the most successful retail chains aimed at kids is the Build-A-Bear Workshop. Customers create their own unique stuffed bears. The stores are based on tweens and their desire for self-expression.

According to Martin Lindstrom's *BRANDchild*, the stores succeed because they meet tweens' values: "let me express myself, let me have fun, let me do my own thing, let me get my friends involved, let me host a great party, let me show off to my friends and family."[1] It is a good example of how a brand name has used the specific wants and needs of a market to be successful.

them distinctive as consumers. While many people perceive advertising to kids as a negative, it focuses on determining and meeting their needs just as advertisers try to meet the needs of adults. According to Martin Lindstrom in *BRANDchild,*

> *Some would prefer that marketers were not allowed to structure advertising campaigns targeting tweens. They perceive marketing to children as exploitation. This is one extreme. But the role of marketing is to create and maintain brands filling a whole variety of needs. In the case of tweens, these include safety, comfort, and let's not forget fun, in all its dimensions.* [2]

Marketers believe that kids deserve product design and advertising specifically intended to meet their needs. This gives them a voice and makes their role in the economy an accepted and important one. With this type of empowerment in the marketplace, kids feel that they can control part of their world as well. According to Juliet Schor in *Born to Buy:*

> *[Advertisers] argue that a sense of control can be achieved through learning how to operate a toy, having the opportunity to choose among products, even something as simple as choosing among color variations, or watching an ad in which children triumph over adults.* [3]

By having a strong voice, young buyers also participate in product development. This allows them a say in creating the kinds of products that best meet their needs. With so much attention focused on their opinions, kids become actively involved in promoting or rejecting products that are targeted to them. This kind of consumer power also helps the market adjust to what kids actually want or need.

CONSUMERS IN TRAINING

In the United States, children are consumers in training. Advertising that specifically targets kids helps them learn to be good consumers. They are inundated with choices for toys, clothing, electronics, and food. Most kids quickly realize that they cannot have everything they see and not every advertisement or product is as good as it is made out to be. To become informed consumers, kids must learn to evaluate products, compare them to other products, and decide what the best value is for their money. They may find this out through trial and error by purchasing less-than-worthwhile products.

Learning to identify and evaluate advertising is also an important consumer skill and one that kids develop from an early age. Although very young children have trouble distinguishing advertisements from regular media, most children and teens are very adept at knowing when someone is trying to sell them something. Some advertisers answer the public's demand for limiting any kind of advertising to kids under a certain age as a disservice. They claim that children who do not see any advertising until the age of 12 or 15 would be unprepared to deal with the sudden barrage of commercials that would bombard them at that point.

Advertisers also observe that kids have become savvier about the accuracy of advertising claims than children were 30 years

The First Amendment

When advertisers and corporations are faced with the idea that they should not market to children, they cite the First Amendment to the Constitution and the right to free speech. Advertisers often contest attempts to limit what they can say and whom they can advertise to as being unconstitutional.

In 1975, the Supreme Court ruled that the First Amendment protected advertisements and other forms of commercial speech. However, they were not protected to the same extent as other forms of speech.

In 1980, the Court handed down another decision that created a test to determine whether restricting a certain type of advertising was permitted by the Constitution. That test includes determining if the commercial speech is not misleading and lawful. The government must show that it would serve the public interest to restrict that particular commercial speech. It must show that the restriction directly advances the interests of the public. And finally, it must show that the restriction is needed to achieve a certain public benefit or purpose.

ago. An advertising employee with the Nickelodeon television channel states, "[K]ids have a kind of truth meter. They are able to tell when marketers are trying to trick them."[4]

Advertisers and marketers point out that children are an important aspect of the national economy. By targeting them and adapting products and services to their specific needs, the market economy ultimately benefits. Production occurs, and people are employed in manufacturing, advertising, and selling those products to kids. In this way, children and teens are a very important piece of the vast machinery of a free-market economy. Advertising prompts them to spend money, and that money benefits other people and their families by creating jobs. In some cases, advertising also pays for the noncommercial content of television programs or magazines. The money that companies spend on print and television ads allows those programs

Interacting Brands

Advertisers who promote their brands with tweens and teens no longer concentrate advertising on just their consumer market. Instead, they have adopted a "Talk Listen Learn React" approach to marketing. They promote the product by talking about it, but then they need to listen to the reaction of their consumers, ask questions about the product, and learn what they can do to improve the product or their advertising approach. Then they can react to the consumer based on their opinions.

Consumers, especially young ones, want to know that their opinions matter. If advertisers listen to their young audience and react by creating or adjusting products, they can inspire brand loyalty.

and publications to exist and provides kids with educational and informational content.

Advertising the Good Stuff

Not all advertising is for products that might be seen as frivolous or completely unhealthy for children and teens. Good products and services can benefit kids, but without targeted advertising, youth consumers might not know about these products.

Educational toys, publications, and other informational products are designed to help kids learn, to encourage their curiosity, or to help them with certain skills. While much of the advertising for strictly educational products is aimed at parents, companies also want kids to be aware of these products and ask for them.

Books are often advertised to kids, especially through methods such as school book fairs sponsored by publishers. This makes a wide selection of books easily available to

Lugnet

The Lego toy company has its best source of marketing information in a Web site that is not actually affiliated with the company. Lugnet.com is an online international community of Lego enthusiasts. They are not paid by the Lego company and are free to say whatever they want about the company and its products. Lego company officials can read comments and interact with their customers on the Web site. This serves as a way to learn what consumers like and dislike as well as a way to get ideas for future products.

kids who might never visit a bookstore. These book fairs are often advertised and promoted with posters, flyers, and even videos that kids watch in their classrooms beforehand. According to Susan Linn in *Consuming Kids*:

> *Book fairs are a time-honored tradition in many schools. While these practices certainly are a form of marketing, many people concerned about advertising in schools have looked the other way because they seemed like a harmless way to get books into children's hands.*[5]

By advertising books and getting kids interested in buying them, marketers are also getting kids excited about reading, a necessary skill. Advertising books is a way to foster the reading habit.

Ethics and Responsibility

Ultimately, the question of whether marketing to kids is positive or negative depends on the methods used by those advertisers. Many feel that marketers are obligated to follow a code of ethics when it comes to marketing to children. For many advertisers, this includes not using violence in advertising or promoting products such as alcohol or cigarettes. Martin Lindstrom notes:

Public Service

Some companies attempt to improve their public image by sponsoring public service announcements. These are similar to commercials except that they exist to encourage or discourage something, such as promoting reading or pointing out the hazards of smoking. On the surface, they are meant solely for the good of the viewing public. However, they also give the sponsoring advertisers an opportunity to be conscientious and community minded. It also provides a means to keep the company's name, brand, or logo in the public's awareness.

Dealing with tweens is like dealing with the future. By affecting them we affect the shape of our future world. . . . There are ethical practices that need to be followed when marketing to young audiences.[6]

David Poltrack, an executive vice president at CBS Television in New York, states:

We accept that children don't have the same kind of built-up resistance to advertising that adults have, so we don't allow the same kinds of things in advertising for kids that we allow for adults. There has to be a level of responsibility.[7]

This kind of responsibility to children in marketing and advertising includes advertising only those products that are of high quality and safe for children. It is also important to maintain truth in advertising and not make false claims that will destroy a child's trust in a product. Advertisers hold each other accountable for being honest about products and not abusing the freedom they have to market products directly to young consumers.

Even companies that create educational products have a responsibility to maintain truth-in-advertising pacts.

Apple has created a number of household brand items, such as the popular iPod.

BRAND CONSCIOUS, FROM BABIES TO TEENS

*B*randing is a form of marketing that tries to foster consumer loyalty to a particular brand. Advertisers want to build brand loyalty among young people that will last throughout their lives.

Children are exposed to brand names from birth. Babies and toddlers might be surrounded by *Sesame Street-* and Disney-themed toys and clothing. Preschoolers want toys and clothes that are linked to their favorite movies and television shows. School children look for products related to television and movie characters or to video games. Teens look for clothing with the current "in" brand-name label. Marketers want to create brands that will become the latest trend.

Is anything wrong with creating brand loyalty? If consumers use a particular brand of soap or toothpaste or coffee and they like it, then they know that brand will satisfy them in the future. But brand names have also become ways to create an elite group of consumers. For example, people who buy expensive coffee from a Starbucks might consider themselves to be more discerning than someone who buys a cup of no-name brand from a convenience store. The same can happen among teens: It can be more appealing to wear clothing from a trendy brand-name boutique than to wear something bought at a discount department store. This applies to electronics, cars, and even food. According to Juliet Schor in *Born to Buy*, teens are increasingly beginning to measure their self-worth in terms of the cost of their belongings:

Branding in Books

Even books written specifically for teen audiences are no longer immune from advertisements and brand-name placement. In June of 2006, Perseus Books Group published the novel *Cathy's Book*, written by Sean Stewart and Jordan Weisman. The story dealt with a 17-year-old girl who was dumped by her boyfriend, which is a typical plot for teen female readers. However, the book became controversial because it incorporated direct references to Cover Girl brand cosmetics and how to use them. Proctor & Gamble, the company that owns Cover Girl, agreed to feature the book on its Web site in exchange for the product placement. According to the company, no money was involved in the agreement. The company also claims that the authors approached them about the deal. Consumer groups such as Commercial Alert protested the deal in a *London Times* article:

> It is not unknown for works of fiction to advance political and other agendas, but this crosses a line. *Cathy's Book* is in the form of a novel. But in reality it is an adjunct of a corporate marketing campaign.[2]

Product placement in adult books is not new. In 2001, the Bulgari jewelry company paid author Fay Weldon to feature its jewelry in her novel *The Bulgari Connection*.

These days, when kids ask, they ask for particular brands. A 2001 Nickelodeon study found that the average ten year old has memorized 300 to 400 brands. Kids have clear brand preferences, they know which brands are cool, they covet them, and they pay attention to the ads for them. Today's tweens are the most brand-conscious generation in history.[1]

Kids are also drawn to brand names because

they want to be more like adults. Wearing kid-sized versions of adult designer clothing or drinking gourmet coffee makes them feel older. Many marketers use the term *aspirational* to describe this trend: aspiring to be older than they are. A teen is an aspirational 20 year old, and a 12 year old might be an aspirational 17 year old. It ties in to the trend of Kids Are Getting Older Younger (KAGOY), and they want the brands to prove it.

THE POWER OF BELONGING

Branding works especially well with tweens and teens because it taps into their desire to belong to a group and be socially accepted. One way of belonging is to wear and possess what everyone else has, especially the trends set by persuader kids. According to Dave Siegel in *The Great Tween Buying Machine*, "Peers become increasingly important as children get older, so they want to know that a product will help them fit in and make them popular."[3]

Certain brands do seem to make kids feel like they fit in with other kids their age. In a survey conducted by the Center for the New American Dream, 62 percent of 12 to 13 year olds said that

Young consumers often wear certain brands to project an image of themselves and to boost self-esteem.

buying certain products made them feel better about themselves. Not everyone can afford to have all the latest brands, however.

THE CONSUMER TRAP

The United States is the most consumer-oriented society in the world. Along with the drive to accumulate stuff, U.S. consumers save less money and have higher levels of credit-card debt. Every year, millions of households declare bankruptcy because of their consumer debt.

Children who have grown up in a consumer culture often place great value on making money. When asked what they want to do when they grow up, most kids focus on making a lot of money rather than finding work that is satisfying and fulfilling. All kids cannot expect to have the same level of income as their parents. If they grow up putting great emphasis on buying, they can expect even more dissatisfaction when they become adults and cannot afford to buy the latest and greatest items.

Even for kids and teens who do keep up with brand trends, the satisfaction is fleeting. According to *Who's Raising Your Child?*, by Laura J. Buddenberg and Kathleen M. McGee,

> *Many teens, in a developmental stage where they are insecure and searching for their own identity, turn to things to define themselves. What most fail to recognize is that acquiring the latest thing rarely brings a lasting happiness. When they become bored with that particular item, the desired result isn't achieved, or the trendy move on to some new fad, teens are left wanting still more. Buying becomes an addiction just like smoking or drinking. They need more and more to feel good, to get a "high."*[4]

Psychologists worry that kids and teens will end up feeling deeply inadequate because they or their families cannot afford a product that they feel is absolutely necessary to their happiness. In a society with an increasing number of poor and low-income households, this is a growing problem.

SELLING WITH SEX AND VIOLENCE

Another major concern about creating and selling brands to kids is the way in which many marketers do it. Kids are often exposed to advertising that glorifies sex and violence to get their message across and sell products. Using violence and sex in advertising is not new. As Susan Linn says in *Consuming Kids*:

> *Sex or sexuality has been exploited since the beginning of advertising to sell everything from cars to candy bars. These days it's also used to sell the media offerings that attract the viewers that marketers want to reach. Ads for TV programs, movies, and music highlight sexual content just as they highlight violence.* [5]

And more and more, kids and teens are the market these advertisers want to reach. By promoting brands that are linked to sexy celebrities or violent

*Fashion and celebrity magazines
influence many girls' clothing choices.*

video games, kids and teens are paying attention and
buying these products.

Girls read fashion and celebrity magazines
at younger and younger ages and look for the
same kinds of sexy, suggestive clothing worn by
the models. Clothing racks in department stores
often feature clothing for young girls that mimics
the suggestive styles of adult clothing as seen in
magazines, movies, and television. Girls yearn to be
"sexy" before they really understand what the word

means, and they want to wear clothing that will give them that quality.

Video games and movies appeal to a taste for violence in many kids and teens, especially boys. Because the violence has appeal, it has found its way into advertising as well. However, because of this appeal, ratings have been created to let parents know what media is appropriate or inappropriate for their children.

Still, video games can be excellent vehicles for embedded advertisements because they can be incorporated into the setting of the game or the characters' actions. Kids remember the thrill of the game and associate the product with that thrill—or as something that helps them belong to a group of kids who like the latest video game. Products directly linked to certain video games, such as action figures, special brands of soda, or clothing, will also sell better because of the association with the appealing game. Television programs such as those that feature professional wrestling are also

Sneaky Ads

In 2000, the Federal Trade Commission (FTC), which monitors television and other media, found that children are still exposed to M-rated video-game advertisements. This rating means that the product is not suitable for those under 17. But the games were subtly advertised through movie theaters, gaming magazines, and other print sources.

popular with kids. Some programs have created their own products, such as action figures and clothing. These items capitalize on kids' fascination with the violence of the program and their desire to emulate that through related products.

Sex and violence sell to adults, and they sell to kids as well. However, even products that kids cannot buy, such as alcohol and cigarettes, are often marketed in ways that will appeal to kids and create consumers-to-be for certain brands. These include alcohol products that taste like sweet, fruity drinks. Kids cannot legally drink them, but they might find the look and colors appealing and will remember the brand (or drink it illegally if the opportunity arises). A vice president of the Nickelodeon television channel explained:

Product preferences develop at a much earlier age than anyone would have ever thought. . . . As people begin to understand

Girls and Cigarettes

According to Susan Linn in *Consuming Kids*, cigarette companies are good at exploiting the fears teenage girls have about their appearance. Even though teens are not supposed to be able to purchase cigarettes, girls often begin smoking as a way to lose weight or keep from gaining weight. When brands of cigarettes specifically targeted at women began to appear in the 1960s, there was an increase in the number of young girls who smoked. Cigarettes can no longer be advertised on television.

this, to see how brand loyalty transfers to adulthood, there is almost nothing that won't be advertised for children.[6]

Does Something Need to Be Done?

Some critics believe that marketing to kids is always bad. And in a consumer culture such as that of the United States, the chances that advertising will decrease or cease to specifically target children are slim. The economy depends on cultivating and encouraging consumerism, and kids are no small part of that.

But does that mean that young consumers and their parents are helpless against the onslaught of marketing directed at them? Or can kids and teens be empowered to be responsible for their own choices as consumers? ⁓

Abercrombie & Fitch has often used sexually provocative images in its advertising campaigns.

*Some students protest different marketing campaigns,
such as the backlash against big tobacco companies.*

LIMITING THE
MARKETING MACHINE

*I*t is not unusual to walk through the halls
of a high school in the United States
and see kids wearing brand-name clothing, shoes,
purses, backpacks, and even sunglasses. But in many
of those high schools, there is a growing movement

referred to as "unbranding." A small but determined group of kids who may have purchased their clothes at a local thrift shop would rather shop there than wear branded clothes. They deliberately avoid the trendiest labels and products. They refuse to be dictated to by corporations and marketers or be "walking billboards" for manufacturer's products.

Students who are actively involved in the unbranding movement often lobby their high schools to get rid of some of the most blatant forms of corporate advertising and sponsorship. Some students have made progress. But what can be done to limit the harmful parts of advertising while keeping the helpful parts?

TELEVISION: THE AD MACHINE

Attempts to limit advertising to children are not new, even in the United States. In the nineteenth century, parents worried that cheap novels, called penny dreadfuls, would corrupt their children. Later, comic books were considered bad for children. Most experts agree that the key to limiting kids' exposure to

An Exercise in Unbranding

Just how much advertising and brand logos are present in daily life? Sit in a room and count how many logos are visible. Look at everything: computer equipment, pens and pencils, mouse pads, books, magazines, food packages, clothing, and mugs. How many logos and brand names are in plain sight?

advertisements targeted especially at them is to limit their television and Internet time. Ideally, they feel that preschoolers should be limited to one hour of television a day. Mark Crispin Miller, a media critic, says:

> *If you watch Saturday morning kids' TV, you can see it in the programming that is unrelievedly frantic, hyped up, hysterical, in its own way quite violent and pervasively commercial. It's all about selling. Now kids grow up in a universe that is utterly suffused with this kind of commercial propaganda. And by that I mean not only the ads per se, but the shows that sell the ads.* [1]

The only way to limit the advertising that very young children see is to either limit their television viewing time or for parents to watch with them and help educate them about what they are seeing in the ads.

Older kids have a wider exposure to media of different types and cannot be limited in the same way as young kids. Parents should still discuss what they are viewing and teach them not to openly accept the claims made by advertisements. Tweens and teens are old enough to take a critical look at advertising. They should be taught to evaluate the many ads that come their way every day and the passing fads at school. It is not easy for adults to discern every form of advertising, since many articles in newspapers, magazines, and on Web sites are actually advertisements. Even public-service announcements on television may subtly advertise the sponsoring companies that create them. Children and teens have a more difficult time telling the difference between advertisements and regular media.

However, parents are not always willing or able to educate their children to look at advertisements aimed specifically at them with a critical eye. For that reason, there have been attempts to limit the number of commercials that kids are exposed to on television. Some foreign countries limit advertising to children. In Sweden, no advertising is permitted during programming intended for children under the age of 12. Greece does not allow advertising for toys to be shown on television during certain times of day. And all ads are banned from

Slow Food

One of the most recent attempts to wean kids away from junk food, fast food, and microwave meals is the "Slow Food" movement. This emphasizes organically grown and locally produced fresh foods. Alice Waters, author of many cookbooks and a restaurant owner, has extended the slow-food idea to schools. She encourages students to grow and prepare their own foods and teaches skills such as menu planning, gardening, harvesting, and composting.

The company TiVo offers options such as KidZone, a filtering system to help parents choose programs that are appropriate for their children.

television in Ireland in the late afternoon, when kids are most likely to be watching.

In the 1950s, the National Broadcasters Association created a code of standards and practices. This was intended, in part, to cope with the need for "respect for the special needs of children [and] for decency and decorum in programming and for propriety in advertising."[2] In the 1970s, the Federal Communications Commission (FCC) banned a practice called host selling. Commercial endorsements for products were built right into television shows and hosts might talk about a certain company or product. In 1983, Congress passed the Children's Television Education Act, which regulated advertising. However, one year later the bans were lifted.

In 1990, the Children's Television Act set limits on advertising but did not limit what products could be advertised. According to Laura J. Buddenberg and Kathleen M. McGee in *Who's Raising Your Child?*:

> The Act restricts commercial time on programs primarily produced for those 12 and younger to 10.5 or 12 minutes per hour depending on the day. Those minutes, however, can pack quite a marketing wallop. We randomly selected one half-hour program running on the WB Network's "Kids Saturday Morning" lineup. Thirty commercials or promos . . . ran in two long sequences during this thirty-minute show.[3]

The biggest obstacle in limiting advertising to children on television is the possible conflicts it creates with the First Amendment right to freedom of speech. The battle continues between those who want to protect children from constant advertising and those who want to make sure that the constitutional rights of advertisers are not being taken away.

LEARNING ABOUT MONEY

Another way in which parents can help their children evaluate advertising and the endless urging to buy products is to educate them about money. In a society saddled with huge amounts of personal debt, kids need to learn that they cannot have everything they want. Ultimately, they have to work for what they do buy. They can be taught to budget their money for items they really want that parents will not necessarily buy for them, such as video-game systems. Kids can learn to manage allowances and perhaps even do extra tasks in order to earn special purchases from their parents. Teens can be limited in how many hours they work a week to avoid impacting their schoolwork. This will also help maintain a healthy balance in their lives, rather than working as much as possible to afford the latest trends and brand names.

Going to the mall has become a form of social activity and leads kids to even more exposure to advertising and products. Shopping has become an acceptable recreational activity for entire families.

Parents may limit recreational shopping for tweens and teens. Replacing it with watching movies, playing games, and other activities that are not tied to spending can help shift the focus away from constant exposure to advertising and purchasing.

Parents can also teach their children not to buy things on a whim. This helps children think about their purchases before they make them. Young consumers have to put some thought into what they want, how much they want it, and why.

A School Walkout

In December of 2001, a group of more than 2,000 students walked out of their private high school in Philadelphia, Pennsylvania. They protested the privatization of their school and others in the area. Edison Schools, Inc. is a New York-based for-profit company that contracts with school districts to operate more than 100 schools in 22 states.

According to Alissa Quart in *Branded*:

First, [the students] see Edison as part of the larger corporate culture that considers young people, and young people of color in particular, just a demographic to be profited from. Second, they see Edison, with its metal detectors and security guards, as the final stage of the increased policing of students.[4]

Students claimed that Edison was trying to set up a school franchise, branding its schools as "Edison Schools," much like a Burger King or a McDonald's. The schools would have blanket policies and educational approaches regardless of their location and student population.

Philadelphia did turn over the management of 20 schools to Edison in 2002, despite the protests from students and adults. But this number was only half of what Edison had originally expected to manage for the school district.

Parents can also encourage their children to be environmentally conscious and consider trading and recycling clothing and toys rather than just buying more new things. Some parents insist that for every new toy or article of clothing a child buys, something already owned must be donated, recycled, or sold.

ADVERTISING IN SCHOOLS

Schools are one of the most difficult areas for change. Most schools do not have enough money and therefore rely heavily on the freebies that advertisers provide in exchange for advertising.

Because of a growing awareness about advertising to kids in school settings, some companies have stopped the practice. In July of 2003, Kraft Foods announced that because of pressure from consumers, it would no longer advertise processed foods on Channel One, the free network provided to students that advertises during its programming.

Many schools have now banned branded vending machines with sodas and junk food from school buildings and replaced them with healthy snacks and bottled water. A growing concern with obesity and the diets of kids and teens has also helped bring changes in schools. Well-known fast-food franchises and vending machines may be limited or removed from school campuses. Some states are even enacting legislation to keep junk foods out of schools.

Kids and their parents can accomplish a great deal in keeping corporate sponsorship and advertising out of their schools, often simply by calling attention to it. Some teens have made the news when they refused to cooperate in company-sponsored school activities.

WHAT IS THE ISSUE?

Many people are resistant to the idea of limited access to certain products. As part of a huge consumer-oriented culture, they believe if kids have the money, they should be able to buy what they want.

Critics argue that there are several reasons for limiting advertising and consumerism for the greater good of kids and teens. One has to do with

Vending Machines

There is a growing controversy over pouring contracts that give a particular brand of soft drinks the right to operate vending machines in a school. Coupled with the increasing concern about the obesity rate among young people, many schools have removed soda vending machines from their buildings.

However in 2003, New York City banned in-school soda machines only to replace them with vending machines for Snapple-brand beverages, some of which contain as much sugar as soda. Snapple paid $8 million to be the official drink of the New York City school system for five years. They claim that they will only sell their brand of water and pure fruit juice.

the effects of the "haves and have-nots," those who can afford trendy brands and new gadgets and those who cannot. According to Alissa Quart in *Branded*, advertising has made the already difficult years of middle and high school even harder for many kids:

> *While fashion, self-adornment and material culture are often fantastic, expressive outlets in themselves, when they are excessively costly, hard-sold and so tantalizing that they occlude minors' other forms of self-hood, they emerge as problems.* [5]

Don't Buy It

Many educational Web sites are attempting to expose marketing ploys and advertising. The Public Broadcasting Service has a Web page for kids called "Don't Buy It" with interactive activities and articles relating to advertising methods and how to combat them as well as how to be a smart consumer.

Encouraging consumerism in kids through targeted advertising has wider implications as well. In a global economy that struggles with environmental problems, do young consumers have a new set of responsibilities? Does having more money and spending opportunities than many other parts of the world mean we should simply continue to buy stuff? ⌐

The pressures caused by new products and advertising can increase
the social divide between different economic classes.

*The United States is a consumer culture
that depends on its free-market economy.*

How Much Stuff
Is Too Much?

mericans are building bigger houses
with more storage space as well as
renting storage facilities at increasing rates. As a
country, the United States has so many consumer
goods that people no longer know what to do with

them. And yet, the United States is part of a global community in which people in developing parts of the world do not have the basics of food, clothing, and shelter. Perhaps one of the biggest arguments against marketing to young people is the need to increase their sense of global responsibility.

THE ANTIGLOBALIZATION MOVEMENT

There have always been people who emphasize the responsible use of resources. But many are unaware of a movement against consumerism and corporate infiltration known as the anti-globalization movement. Within this movement, there are many issues. One aspect is the fight against huge corporations that seek to spread their corporate culture throughout the world. For example, McDonald's has opened franchises all over the world. Antiglobalization proponents argue that this type of global commercial culture detracts from the individuality of countries and cultures. It also negatively affects their economies by taking away business from local companies.

More Stuff

A commercial produced in the 1990s by a plastic storage box company showed a family standing in a room filled with toys, clothing, and household goods. The family purchased plastic containers to store everything in, then looked around the now-empty room and said, "Hey! We need more stuff!"

This movement can be linked to the anti-consumerism movement. Concerned citizens protest against mindless buying and the way that consumers are treated by the market economy. They argue that people no longer value goods and services for what they really are. Instead, people buy goods and services for what they represent and how they might enhance the buyer's social status. An example might be to own an expensive car or a fur coat to indicate wealth and social status rather than as a means of transportation or keeping warm.

But how does limiting

Buy Nothing Day

The United States is the largest consumer of agricultural and natural materials in the world. The American Association for the Advancement of Science's Atlas of Population and Environment tracks who uses various commodities. Out of the 20 major traded commodities, the United States takes the greatest share of 11 of them: corn, coffee, copper, lead, zinc, tin, aluminum, rubber, oil seeds, oil, and natural gas.

According to its Web site, the *Adbusters* magazine's major concern is "the erosion of our physical and cultural environments by commercial forces."[1] Each year, the magazine sponsors a Buy Nothing Day event. In the United States, the Buy Nothing Day usually takes place on the day after Thanksgiving that is a traditional major pre-Christmas shopping day. The Buy Nothing Day is a protest against consumerism. Participants are urged not to buy anything on that day as a way to begin a new attitude toward consumption in general. Although *Adbusters* tries to buy airtime on television stations such as MTV to promote this event, many major networks refuse to air their ads for fear of upsetting their paid retail advertisers.

consumerism in the United States and glorifying it less with young people help the wider global community? Producing consumer goods requires resources, both in raw materials and in energy to manufacture those goods. These resources are becoming increasingly limited. Should U.S. consumers and others in developed countries use the major share of these global resources just to support a consumer lifestyle?

SHARING RESOURCES

According to Anup Shah in an article on the Global Issues Web site on waste and resources:

> We see from the [United Nations] statistics . . . that the world's wealthiest 20 percent consume 86 percent of the world's resources while the poorest 20 percent consume just a miniscule 1.3 percent, that it is not most of the world consuming the resources.[2]

Shah argues that Western cultures based on consumerism use too much of the world's environmental resources. These cultures also create wasteful spending that could be used to help some of the most poverty-stricken nations in the world have a better standard of living.

Children growing up in the United States are bombarded by advertisements for products deemed necessary to be popular and part of the group. However, these products can impact the lives of people on the other side of the world. It takes many resources in raw goods, energy, and people to manufacture the items that may be used for a few months and then discarded. Those who criticize advertising to children argue that by minimizing the marketing and changing attitudes about consumerism, the worldwide economy will benefit. The change could be as small as every kid in the United States buying one less product each month.

But as long as kids are surrounded by traditional advertising as well as embedded products, brand recognition, product contracts in the schools, and parents who spend more than they earn, the culture of consumerism will continue to thrive. And that has had enormous implications for the general health of society.

THE DEBT MONSTER

Seventy-five years ago, average U.S. citizens rarely had large amounts of debt. If they wanted or needed something, they either purchased it with

Increased use of credit cards has led many Americans to carry a heavy load of consumer debt.

cash or went without until they had saved the money for it. For large purchases, such as cars, "paying on time" became a new way to finance a purchase. The consumer borrowed money to purchase costly items and paid it back with monthly payments plus interest. Today, most people use credit cards for everyday items, major purchases such as televisions, and impulse items. People are spending more using credit cards and paying it back at a large rate of interest.

Many economists worry that consumer debt from credit cards has reached an uncontrollable rate. According to Kim Khan in an article on the MSN

Money Web site:

> *About 43% of American families spend more than they earn each year. Average households carry some $8,000 in credit card debt. American consumers owed a grand total of $1.9773 trillion in October 2003, according to statistics on consumer credit from the Federal Reserve.*[3]

People are getting more credit cards at earlier ages (some as teens or college students). Is it wise to keep encouraging kids to spend as much money as they can by targeting them with more and more advertisements?

Everyone has a choice. Just because advertising surrounds kids and teens every day does not mean that they cannot be savvy enough to make good purchasing choices. The unbranding movement is a positive sign. Young consumers do not have to be influenced by corporations and advertisers. Through responsible exposure to consumer goods, kids and teens can become wise consumers. Being a consumer does not just mean *consuming* goods. It also means questioning a company's product and how it is promoted. This includes the choice not to make purchases. Even the youngest consumers can speak through their wallets by spending or not spending.

Responsible consumers make informed purchases based on needs rather than impulse buys based on wants.

TIMELINE

1400s–1500s

Printed handbills are used for advertising.

1600s

The first advertisements appear in English weekly newspapers.

1841

The first advertising agency is created.

1934

The Communications Act creates the Federal Communication Commission (FCC).

1950s

The practice of selling ads to multiple sponsors on television begins.

1960s

Advertisers begin creating new and innovative ads that sell an idea or a feeling as well as a product.

Late 1800s	1914	1920s
Branding begins as a way to link products with quality.	The Federal Trade Commission (FTC) is created and regulates advertising, packaging, and labeling.	Advertisers sponsor radio programs with ads.

1969	1975	1979
The first program-length cartoon advertisement for kids airs.	The Supreme Court rules that commercial speech is at least partially covered by the First Amendment.	The first McDonald's Happy Meal goes on sale.

TIMELINE

1982	1983	1984
Reese's Pieces candy is the first product placement in movies and television.	Congress passes the Children's Television Education Act to regulate advertising in children's television.	The ban on program-length commercials for children is lifted.

2000	2001
Author Naomi Klein publishes *No Logo*.	The Motherhood Project issues its "Watch Out for Children" statement to advertisers.

1989

Channel One begins in schools. It requires that commercials are shown in exchange for free television equipment.

1990

The Children's Television Act of 1990 requires broadcasters to show three hours of children's educational programming per week.

1992

The first Buy Nothing Day occurs in Canada.

2003

New York City bans soda vending machines in schools but signs a deal with Snapple beverages to supply them instead.

2007

McDonald's spends $1,600 to pay for printing Happy Meal coupons on report card envelopes in Seminole County, Florida.

Essential Facts

At Issue

Children, tweens, and teens are among the most sought-after advertising markets because of how much money they have to spend. The average child views, hears, or reads more than 40,000 commercials a year. New media technology such as cell phones, the Internet, and advertising venues in schools have made it possible for advertisers to place commercials in every aspect of children's lives. Meanwhile, the "unbranding" movement among teens is a reaction to consumerism and focuses on refusing to use products that are dictated by fashion trends and advertising.

In Favor

❖ Marketing directly to kids may empower them by giving them a say in product development, teaching shopping and consumer skills, and focusing attention on educational and beneficial products.

❖ To become responsible consumers, kids should be educated about consumer skills. This includes advertising and how advertisers entice them to buy.

❖ Young consumers need to look closely at their spending habits and product options as well as their global responsibility in order to fight back against consumerism.

Opposed

❖ Food marketing in schools is a direct link to the obesity epidemic.

❖ Linking foods, toys, and clothing for kids to current movies or cartoon characters encourages them to buy these things or pester their parents for them.

❖ The consumer culture in the United States contributes to the fact that the country uses more resources than other countries and has an unfair share of raw materials and money.

CRITICAL DATES

1950s
Advertisers began selling products through multiple sponsors on television. Children were also exposed to advertising through radio serials.

1980s
Congress first regulated, then deregulated, advertising directed at children, upholding First Amendment rights to free speech. The advertising industry reacted by beginning to more closely monitor itself and its actions.

2003
Some school districts, including New York City's, began to leave their pouring contracts with soda companies and other snack-food vendors. Throughout the first decade of the twenty-first century, wider movements began to occur toward unbranding and more responsible consumerism.

QUOTES

"Kids have very little control over the world in which they live. Therefore, they love to gain a measure of control over their sphere of existence. . . . Control touches a strong need that children have to be independent." —*Gene del Vecchio*

"Many teens, in a developmental stage where they are insecure and searching for their own identity, turn to things to define themselves. What most fail to recognize is that acquiring the latest thing rarely brings a lasting happiness." —*Laura J. Buddenberg and Kathleen M. McGee*

ADDITIONAL RESOURCES

SELECT BIBLIOGRAPHY

Buddenberg, Laura J., and Kathleen M. McGee. *Who's Raising Your Child? Battling the Marketers for Your Child's Heart and Soul*. Boys Town, NE: Boys' Town Press, 2004.

Linn, Susan. *Consuming Kids: Protecting Our Children from the Onslaught of Marketing & Advertising*. New York: Random House, 2005.

Quart, Alissa. *Branded: The Buying and Selling of Teenagers*. New York: Perseus Books Group, 2003.

Schor, Juliet B. *Born to Buy*. New York: Scribner, 2005.

FURTHER READING

Mayr, Diane. *The Everything Kids' Money Book: From Saving to Spending to Investing—Learn All About Money!* Holbrook, MA: Adams Media Corporation, 2002.

Mierau, Christina. *Accept No Substitutes: The History of American Advertising*. Minneapolis, MN: Lerner Books, 2000.

Milton, Bess. *Advertising*. New York: Children's Press, 2004.

Web Links

To learn more about advertising, visit ABDO Publishing Company on the World Wide Web at **www.abdopublishing.com**. Web sites about advertising to children are featured on our Book Links page. These links are routinely monitored and updated to provide the most current information available.

For More Information

For more information on this subject, contact or visit the following organizations.

The Advertising Icon Museum
4600 Madison Avenue, Suite 1500, Kansas City, MO 64112
www.advertisingiconmuseum.com
Open in Spring 2009, this museum is dedicated to the icons and characters that have become household names through advertising.

The Eisner American Museum of Advertising and Design
208 North Water Street, Milwaukee, WI 53202
414-847-3290
www.eisnermuseum.org
This interactive center studies the impact of design and advertising on society as well as its historical and cultural significance.

Library of Congress American Memory Collection
101 Independence Avenue Southeast, Washington DC 20540
202-707-8000
Collections also available online:
memory.loc.gov/ammem/browse/ListSome.
php?category=Advertising
These collections take viewers through the history of advertising and media, including its emergence in the United States.

GLOSSARY

brand loyalty
When a consumer likes a brand-name product and will continue to buy that brand.

branding
The process of getting consumers to become attached and loyal to specific brands according to their age or group.

cater
To provide or supply what is needed by a specific person or group.

conjunction
Together with or in combination with someone or something.

consumerism
The state of practicing an increasing consumption of goods and services.

demographic
A particular statistical group, as determined by divisions, such as age, sex, or income.

disposable income
The part of someone's income left over after bills and taxes are paid, which they can spend freely.

elusive
Evasive, hard to grasp or understand.

encompass
To include, envelop, or surround completely.

ethics
Moral principles or values, a code of behavior.

franchise
A store or restaurant that is locally owned and operated but is part of a large national chain.

icon
A picture, image, symbol, or representation of a company. A cartoon character is an example of an icon.

intrusive
Pushing in without welcome or invitation.

inundated
Overwhelmed.

materialistic
Preoccupied with material objects or with collecting and possessing goods.

naming rights
When a company pays a fee for the right to name a place after that company, as a form of advertising.

nonconformist
A person who refuses to follow the established customs, ideas, or practices of their group.

obese
An extremely overweight person.

placement
Arrangement, location, or placing something in a specific location in order to attract attention to it.

preferences
Choices, as in something preferred over something else.

promotion
Something like a contest or a commercial designed to publicize and advertise a product.

reflexive
Reflecting others' behavior and conforming to that same behavior.

repercussions
Effects or results of some event or action.

savvy
Experienced, well informed, and knowledgeable.

tactic
A plan or procedure for accomplishing a specific goal.

Source Notes

Chapter 1. Marketing 101

1. Susan Linn. *Consuming Kids: Protecting Our Children from the Onslaught of Marketing & Advertising*. New York: Random House, 2005. 1.

2. "The Producer's Corner." Media Education Foundation. 15 Mar. 2006. Motherhood Project interview. 22 Apr. 2008 <http://www.mediaed.org/news/articles/ProducersCornerAdrianaBarbaro>.

3. Martin Lindstrom. *BRANDchild*. Sterling, VA: Kogan Page Ltd., 2003. 1–2.

4. "The Producer's Corner." Media Education Foundation. 15 Mar. 2006. Motherhood Project interview. 22 Apr. 2008 <http://www.mediaed.org/news/articles/ProducersCornerAdrianaBarbaro>.

5. Juliet B. Schor. *Born to Buy*. New York: Scribner, 2005. 9.

6. Laura J. Buddenberg and Kathleen M. McGee. *Who's Raising Your Child? Battling the Marketers for Your Child's Heart and Soul*. Boys Town, NE: Boys' Town Press, 2004. 3.

7. Juliet B. Schor. *Born to Buy*. New York: Scribner, 2005. 179.

Chapter 2. A History of Kids as Consumers

1. Juliet B. Schor. *Born to Buy*. New York: Scribner, 2005. 25.

2. Children's Advertising Review Unit Web site. 2003. 10 Apr. 2008 <http://www.caru.org/>.

3. Laura J. Buddenberg and Kathleen M. McGee. *Who's Raising Your Child? Battling the Marketers for Your Child's Heart and Soul*. Boys Town, NE: Boys' Town Press, 2004. 6.

4. Susan Linn. *Consuming Kids: Protecting Our Children from the Onslaught of Marketing & Advertising*. New York: Random House, 2005. 1.

5. Martin Lindstrom. *BRANDchild*. Sterling, VA: Kogan Page Ltd., 2003. xxv.

Chapter 3. Marketing to Kids Today

1. Martin Lindstrom. *BRANDchild*. Sterling, VA: Kogan Page Ltd., 2003. 15–16.
2. Juliet B. Schor. *Born to Buy*. New York: Scribner, 2005. 56.
3. Girls Intelligence Agency. 2004. 30 May 2008 <http://www.girlsintelligenceagency.com/>.
4. Alissa Quart. *Branded: The Buying and Selling of Teenagers*. New York: Perseus Books Group, 2003. 64.
5. Martin Lindstrom. *BRANDchild*. Sterling, VA: Kogan Page Ltd., 2003. 151.

Chapter 4. Food Marketing

1. Susan Linn. *Consuming Kids: Protecting Our Children from the Onslaught of Marketing & Advertising*. New York: Random House, 2005. 97.
2. Ibid. 100.
3. Juliet B. Schor. *Born to Buy*. New York: Scribner, 2005. 64.
4. Frank Swoboda. "Pepsi Prank Fizzles at School's Coke Day." *Washington Post*. 26 Mar. 1998. 7 May 2008 <http://www.ibiblio.org/commercialfree/presscenter/art_32698.html>.

Chapter 5. Creating Savvy Consumers

1. Martin Lindstrom. *BRANDchild*. Sterling, VA: Kogan Page Ltd., 2003. n. pag.
2. Ibid. 315.
3. Juliet B. Schor. *Born to Buy*. New York: Scribner, 2005. 179.
4. Ibid. 180.
5. Susan Linn. *Consuming Kids: Protecting Our Children from the Onslaught of Marketing & Advertising*. New York: Random House, 2005. 91.
6. Martin Lindstrom. *BRANDchild*. Sterling, VA: Kogan Page Ltd., 2003. n. pag.
7. Miriam H. Zoll. "Psychologists Challenge Ethics of Marketing to Children." American News Service. 5 Apr. 2000. <http://www.mediachannel.org/originals/kidsell.shtml>. 4.

Source Notes continued

Chapter 6. Brand Conscious, from Babies to Teens

1. Juliet B. Schor. *Born to Buy*. New York: Scribner, 2005. 25.
2. Dalya Alberge. "Teen Novel Is Given the Corporate Make Over." 21 June 2006. Commercial Alert Web site. 2 June 2008 <http://www.commercialalert.org/news/Archive/2006/06/teen-novel-is-given-the-corporate-make-over>.
3. Susan Linn. *Consuming Kids: Protecting Our Children from the Onslaught of Marketing & Advertising*. New York: Random House, 2005. 111.
4. Laura J. Buddenberg and Kathleen M. McGee. *Who's Raising Your Child? Battling the Marketers for Your Child's Heart and Soul*. Boys Town, NE: Boys' Town Press, 2004. 19.
5. Susan Linn. *Consuming Kids: Protecting Our Children from the Onslaught of Marketing & Advertising*. New York: Random House, 2005. 128.
6. Ibid. 131.

Chapter 7. Limiting the Marketing Machine

1. Robert McChesney, "Merchants of Cool: What's This Doing to Kids?", PBS Frontline, p.6. <http://www.pbs.org/wgbh/pages/frontline/shows/cool/themes/doingtokids.html>.
2. Susan Linn. *Consuming Kids: Protecting Our Children from the Onslaught of Marketing & Advertising*. New York: Random House, 2005. 147.
3. Laura J. Buddenberg and Kathleen M. McGee. *Who's Raising Your Child? Battling the Marketers for Your Child's Heart and Soul*. Boys Town, NE: Boys' Town Press, 2004. 29.
4. Alissa Quart. *Branded: The Buying and Selling of Teenagers*. New York: Perseus Books Group, 2003. n. pag.
5. Ibid. 230–231.

Chapter 8. How Much Stuff Is Too Much?

1. "About Adbusters." Adbusters: The Media Foundation Web site. 7 May 2008 <http://www.adbusters.org/network/about_us.php>.

2. Anup Shah. "Beyond Consumption and Consumerism: Wasted Wealth, Capital, Labor and Resources." globalissues.org Web site, 23 Sept. 2001. 25 Apr. 2008 <http://www.globalissues.org/TradeRelated/Consumption/Waste.asp>.

3. Kim Khan. "The Basics: How Does Your Debt Compare?" MSN Money Web site. 25 Apr. 2008 <http://moneycentral.msn.com/content/SavingandDebt/P70581.asp>.

INDEX

About the Author

Marcia Amidon Lusted is the author of 12 books for children. She is also a writing instructor and an editorial assistant for Cobblestone Publishing. She lives in New Hampshire.

Photo Credits

Scott Erskine/AP Images, cover; Image Source/AP Images, 6, 54, 88, 93; Mark Lennihan/AP Images, 9; Nick Ut/AP Images, 15; Reed Saxon/AP Images, 17; Anthony Camerano/AP Images, 18; AP Images, 29; Damian Dovarganes/AP Images, 22; Al Behrman/AP Images, 24; Javier Pierini/AP Images, 30; Lauren Greenfield/AP Images, 32; Jae C. Hong/AP Images, 41; Keith Srakocic/AP Images, 42; Larry Crowe/AP Images, 45; Peter Barreras/AP Images, 48; Steve Miller/AP Images, 53; Marcio Jose Sanchez/AP Images, 63, 64; Toyokazu Kosugi/AP Images, 68; Katsumi Kasahara/AP Images, 71; Paul Sakuma/AP Images, 75; Linda Spillers/AP Images, 76; Kathy Willens/AP Images, 80; Via Productions/AP Images, 86; Danny Johnston/AP Images, 95